D1315001

A Nature Walk in the City

Louise and Richard Spilsbury

Heinemann
LIBRARY

Chicago, Illinois

Edited by Joanna Issa, Penny West, Krissy Mohn,
and Gina Kammer
Designed by Cynthia Akiyoshi
Picture research by Elizabeth Alexander
and Tracy Cummins
Production by Helen McCreath
Originated by Capstone Global Library Ltd
Printed and bound in China by Leo Paper Group

18 17 16 15 14
10 9 8 7 6 5 4 3 2 1

Library of Congress Cataloging-in-Publication Data
Cataloging-in-publication information is on file with the
Library of Congress.

ISBN 978-1-4846-0401-4 (hardcover)
ISBN 978-1-4846-0406-9 (eBook PDF)

Acknowledgments
We would like to thank the following for permission to
reproduce photographs:

Alamy: © Julia Gavin, 18, © sandy young, 20, © Washington
Imaging, 6; Getty Images: Ditto, front cover; iStock: ©
txe, 15, back cover; naturepl.com: Laurent Geslin, 14,
Meul/ARCO, 17, Nick Upton/2020VISION, 13, Terry
Whittaker/2020VISION, 19, 21; Shutterstock: ajt, design
element (slug), Alex Staroseltsev, design element (ladybug),
Eric Isselee, design element (fox), Evgeniy Ayupov, design
element (ant), evronphoto, 5, Iain McGillivray, 9, James
Laurie, 16, landysh, 10, Martin Horsky, design element
(stone pavement), Mary Rice, design element (bricks),
mycteria, design element (cobblestone), Nadiia Korol, 22
top left, oBatchenko, front cover, back cover, Oleksiy Mark,
22 bottom left, Pakhnyushcha, design element (rat), PHOTO
FUN, 12 inset, Quang Ho, design element (flower), romrf,
22 bottom right, Sergii Figurnyi, 4, T Cassidy, 22 top right,
Tomatito, 11, Valerie Potapova, 8, Voyagerix, 7, back cover
left, zebra0209, 12, zhangyang13576997233, design
element (leaf)

We would like to thank Michael Bright for his assistance in
the preparation of this book.

Every effort has been made to contact copyright holders
of material reproduced in this book. Any omissions will be
rectified in subsequent printings if notice is given to the
publisher.

All the Internet addresses (URLs) given in this book were
valid at the time of going to press. However, due to the
dynamic nature of the Internet, some addresses may have
changed, or sites may have changed or ceased to exist
since publication. While the author and publisher regret any
inconvenience this may cause readers, no responsibility for
any such changes can be accepted by either the author or
the publisher.

006994LeoF14

Contents

Some words are shown in bold, **like this**. You can find out what they mean by looking in the glossary.

Where are we going?

We are going for a nature walk in the city. There are lots of plants and animals in a city if you know where to look.

When you walk in a city, watch out for traffic. Do not walk and look for wildlife at the same time. Be safe—stop and then look!

What is up on the roof?

Use binoculars to look up at the roof. Can you see herring gulls and their **nests** there? When the eggs **hatch**, parent gulls feed the chicks scraps of food found in trash cans.

Can you spot a pigeon collecting plastic straws or other trash? Pigeons often use these things to make nests. They live off scraps of food that they find in the street.

What grows on the street?

Can you see leaves on the street? They come from trees that grow here. People create areas of soil that trees can grow in among the hard concrete and asphalt streets.

Look at a tree trunk. The **bark** around a tree protects the living plant inside. A sycamore tree's bark flakes off so the trunk does not get clogged up with **pollution** and dirt.

What lives in parks?

Look for clues about what lives in parks. Can you see any animals or insects moving in the trees or gardens?

Squirrels run up and down trees to look for food. They save the food to eat in winter. Their big front teeth help them to break open nutshells to eat the seeds inside.

What lives on walls?

Young ivy plants have floppy **stems** but can climb up walls. Look for the small **roots** that grow out of the ivy stem. These grow into the wall and hold up the plant.

roots

Look closely at the ivy leaves and flowers. Lots of insects feed on the **nectar** inside the ivy's pale flowers. Spiders spin webs to catch insects to eat.

Is the sidewalk empty?

Is there a silvery trail on the sidewalk?
A snail or a slug is nearby. Snails and slugs
make trails of slimy **mucus**. The trails help
them glide across the ground to look for food.

Can you see ants carrying tiny bits of food across the sidewalk? Some ants collect food to take back to their **nests**. They share it with the other ants in their groups.

What lives in the bushes?

Use a magnifying glass to spot insects in the bushes. Insect mouths are shaped to help them eat. Can you see a butterfly's curly **proboscis** sucking **nectar** juice from flowers?

Look for ladybugs with their red and black spots. A ladybug has a hard mouth for crunching tiny insects. Its bright colors warn birds that it will taste bad if they eat it.

What animals come out at night?

Look for clues about animals that come out at night. Which animal digs holes like this?

Foxes dig holes called **dens** under sheds or bushes. They have their babies in dens. Foxes eat scraps of meat and other food that they find on the street or in trash cans.

19

How can I protect city animals?

Protect city wildlife by putting litter in the trash. Litter can harm animals. They can choke on plastic bags or get trapped inside empty jars.